YOUTH SPECIALTIES CLIP-ART BOOK

Featuring the artwork of

Dave Ball
Craig Boldman
Rick Bundschuh
Jack Fuller
Doug Hall

Koko Herschberger
Corbin Hillam
Nick Hobart
Eric & Vicki Johnson
Linda Lafond

Mark Lindelius
Dan Pegoda
Michael Streff
Robert Suggs
Craig McNair Wilson

Edited by
Wayne Rice

Book Design by
Gary Bell and Jerry Jamison

Cover Design by
Corbin Hillam

Youth Specialties

ZONDERVAN PUBLISHING HOUSE
Grand Rapids, Michigan

THE YOUTH SPECIALTIES CLIP ART BOOK

Youth Specialties Books are published by Zondervan
Publishing House, 1415 Lake Drive, S.E.,
Grand Rapids, Michigan 49506

First printing   1985
First Zondervan printing   1985
ISBN 0-310-34911-7

88 89 90 / 10 9 8 7 6 5

CONTENTS

HOW TO USE YOUR

YOUTH SPECIALTIES CLIP ART BOOK

YOUR YOUTH SPECIALTIES Clip Art Book contains hundreds of drawings, cartoons, borders and other pieces of art that you can use to produce inexpensive, yet attractive, printed materials for your youth group. You can use this artwork on:

- Mailers
- Handouts
- Tickets
- Fliers
- Brochures
- Posters
- Letterheads
- Bulletins
- Programs
- Overhead Transparencies
- Greeting Cards
- Newsletters
- Forms
- Newspaper Ads
- T-shirt designs
- Book Covers
- Bumper Stickers

Most youth workers are not professional artists (if you are, you are a rare exception), but almost every youth worker needs to be able to produce professional-looking artwork from time to time. The following simple steps, plus this book, will enable you to do just that.

To begin, you will need to get some basic art supplies. By improvising, you can get by without all of them, but you shouldn't handicap yourself just to save a few dollars. Most of these items are worth the small investment that is required:

1. A sharp pair of scissors
2. An "X-acto" knife, with a #11 blade

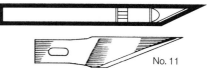
No. 11

3. A ruler, preferably one with a metal straight-edge
4. A pencil (and a pencil sharpener)
5. A light blue (non-reproducing) pen or pencil
6. An eraser
7. Some rubber cement

8. A roll of masking tape (about ½ inch wide)
9. A roll of scotch tape (clear)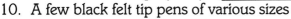
10. A few black felt tip pens of various sizes
11. Some "white-out" (Liquid Paper correction fluid)

Here are some optional materials, if you really want to get serious about doing first class artwork:

12. A drafting table or portable desk top drawing board
13. A t-square or "parallel rule"

14. A 30 degree triangle (clear), or an "adjustable" triangle. (Your drawing board, t-square and triangle will insure that everything will be perfectly straight both vertically and horizontally. This will help to insure that "professional" look.)

15. An electric "waxer" (for sticking things down—replaces rubber cement)
16. Sheets of "transfer lettering" (rub-on type. You can buy almost any style in big sheets which can be used for headlines and other applications. It is relatively expensive, but it goes a long way and makes your artwork look good. Some common brands are "Formatt," "Zipatone" and "Letraset." Most art stores will carry several brands and will give you a catalog displaying all the different styles that are available).
17. A "burnishing tool"—a flat surface for rubbing down artwork and transfer lettering.
18. Technical pens, for drawing fine or fat lines (Ask your art dealer about these. Technical pens will give you a "cleaner" line than felt tips.)

PREPARING ARTWORK FOR THE PRINTER

ASSUMING THAT YOU HAVE a minimum amount of supplies to get going, here's a simple procedure for putting together a finished piece of artwork for the printer.

1. Get a blank sheet of white paper, or better yet, a piece of stiff white card stock ("stock" is another word for paper in printer's jargon). This will be your "paste-up board" (more jargon). It should be the same size as the final product will be, although sometimes it's a good idea to use a little larger piece of paper or card to give you some extra margin to work with.

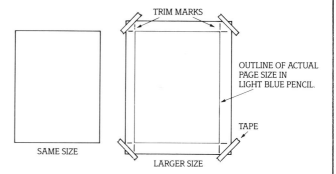

TRIM MARKS

OUTLINE OF ACTUAL PAGE SIZE IN LIGHT BLUE PENCIL.

TAPE

SAME SIZE

LARGER SIZE

If you prefer, you can prepare your artwork much larger than the final product and ask the printer to "reduce" it to the size you want. This will allow you to work "big" so that you can get in more information or detail. When the artwork is reduced, everything will be smaller—even the width of your lines.

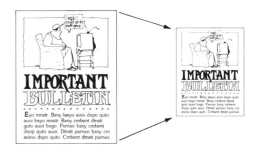

This also allows you to use the same artwork for more than one application. For example, it could be used as a poster and also as a small handout.

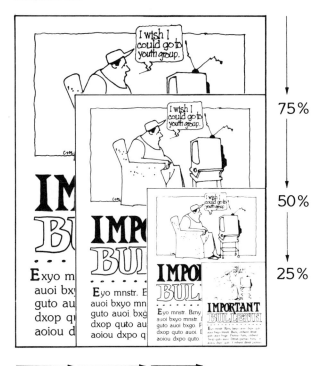

75%

50%

25%

Keep in mind that if you do this, your artwork will reduce both horizontally and vertically. You'll need to prepare your artwork accordingly.

2. Next, you will need to compose your "copy" (what you want to say). If it is an announcement, you'll probably want a catchy headline, along with the details—what, where, when, how much will it cost, etc.

It is usually a good idea at this point to decide which things you want to highlight as well. In other words, you may want to put certain things in larger letters, or put a border around especially important information.

3. Now, scan the contents of this book and locate the artwork that you think will best compliment your "copy." Most of the art in this book is provided in several sizes to give you some flexibility in designing your page layout. It is also printed on one side of the paper, so that you can cut it out without destroying anything on the other side.

Carefully clip the art from the book (now you know why it's called a "clip art" book) with your scissors or your "X-acto" knife. If you use the latter, make sure you don't cut through several pages at once. Be sure to leave some white paper around the artwork that you remove from the book. In other words, don't cut it out right on the lines.

4. Now, "lay-out" your page design. Put the clip art on the page where you want it and decide where your "copy" (headlines, details) will go. You can sketch this on your paste-up board (the paper/card described in step #1) with your blue, non-reproducing pencil, or you can do it on a separate sheet of paper. If you do this, you will avoid problems like running out of room for your headlines.

WRONG (result of not sketching layout ahead of time)

RIGHT (result of proper planning by sketching layout first)

5. Prepare your "copy" artwork by hand-lettering it with black felt-tip pens, a black typewriter, transfer lettering, or some other method. As long as it is black, red, or some other dark color, it will reproduce. You can do this directly on the paste-up board, or you can do it on separate sheets of paper which can then be pasted-up into position.

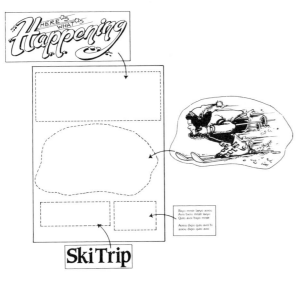

Your copy can also be "typeset" at a professional typesetter or print shop. It will look similar to the copy that you are reading right now—very slick, neat, and professional. Although this is usually expensive, it can sometimes be worth it. Your local printer or typesetter can explain to you the procedures involved in typesetting, and the cost.

6. Once you've decided where everything will go, put it all together (do your "paste-up"). Everything can be pasted down into position using rubber cement. Rubber cement works best because it is not permanent (you can change your mind) and it's easy to clean up. Don't use "white" glue or adhesive sprays. Clear Scotch tape can be used, but you'll want to make sure your hands are clean or you'll have fingerprints taped down as well as your artwork.

Try to keep everything as straight as possible (use your T-square if you have one) and neat (wash your hands and don't sit coffee cups on your artwork). The better your pasted-up artwork looks, the better your final product will look. Printers can't always make smudges and crooked lines disappear.

AND SPEAKING OF PRINTERS ...

THERE ARE A VARIETY of good ways to get things printed up. Some are expensive, but most are quite inexpensive.

If you want your final product to look as professional as possible, have it printed by the "offset" method of printing. (This book is printed that way.) Most print shops do this and prices vary greatly, depending on the equipment, the job requirements, and so on. Shop around for the best deal. If you are doing a simple 8½ by 11 flyer, printed in one color (like black ink on white or colored stock) use a "fast-print" shop, such as "Postal Instant Press (P.I.P.)," "Sir Speedy," or

"Quick-Print." Such a print shop can give you excellent quality and fast service at very reasonable prices. They are usually able to handle special requirements like reductions, printing on both sides of a sheet, folding, and the like without any difficulty.

If you need something more complicated, like printing photographs, several colors, odd-sized sheet sizes, etc., you may need to use a larger, better-equipped print shop. Always take your artwork and your job specifications to several printers and ask for "bids" on the job.

If you only need a small quantity, or if you need something very quickly, then you might find it best to use a plain-paper copier rather than a print shop. Most copiers now offer excellent quality reproductions in a variety of colors, and are capable of reductions and printing on both sides of the page. If you use the copier method of printing, make sure your original artwork is as clean as possible, eliminating any shadows which might reproduce.

HAVE FUN!

CORBIN HILLAM

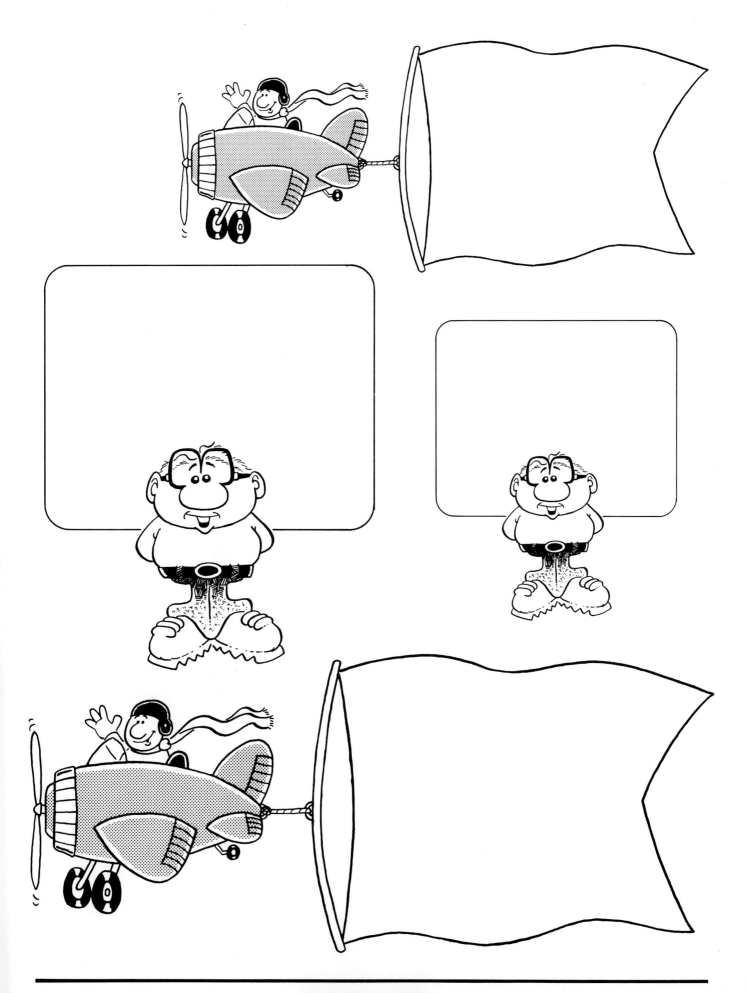

BE THERE

BE THERE

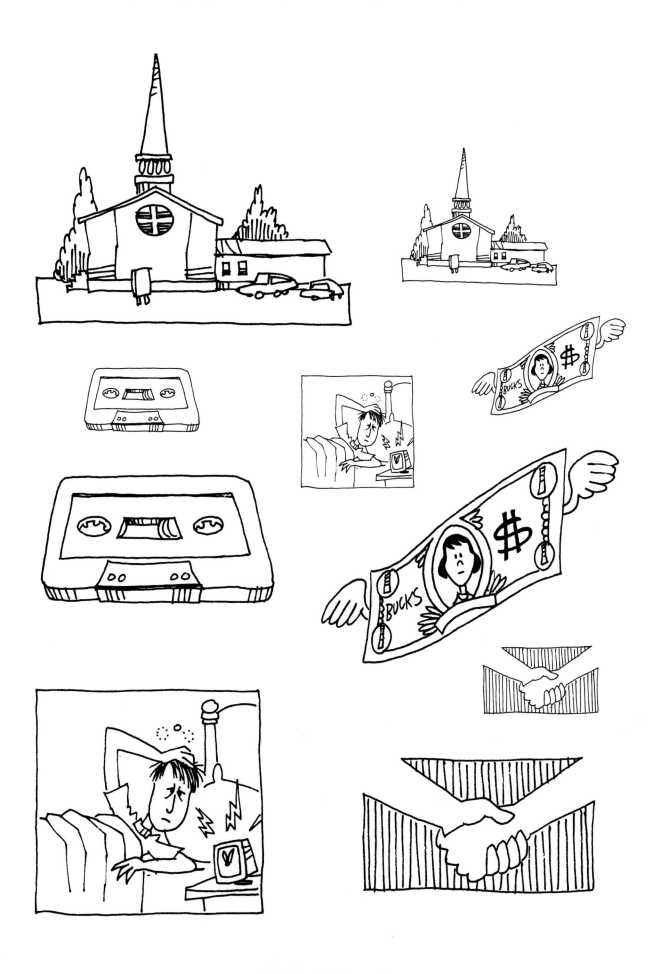

DON'T FORGET:

DON'T FORGET:

"Conformity"

"Tired Of Hanging Around
With The Same Old Birdbrains?"

- HAPPY BIRTHDAY -

- HAPPY BIRTHDAY -

YOUTH SPECIALTIES
CLIP-ART

"Bible Study"

"Back To School"

"Prayer"

"Peer Pressure"

"Self-Image"

"Missions"

"Choir"

"Babysitting"

"Bundle Up"

"Senior Citizens"

"Self-Image"

"Serving Others"

"Feeling A Little Down?"

"Homework"

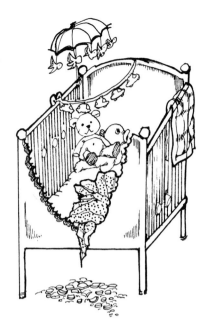

"Children/Babysitting"

"Self-Image"

"Worn Out?"

"Love"

"Substance Abuse"

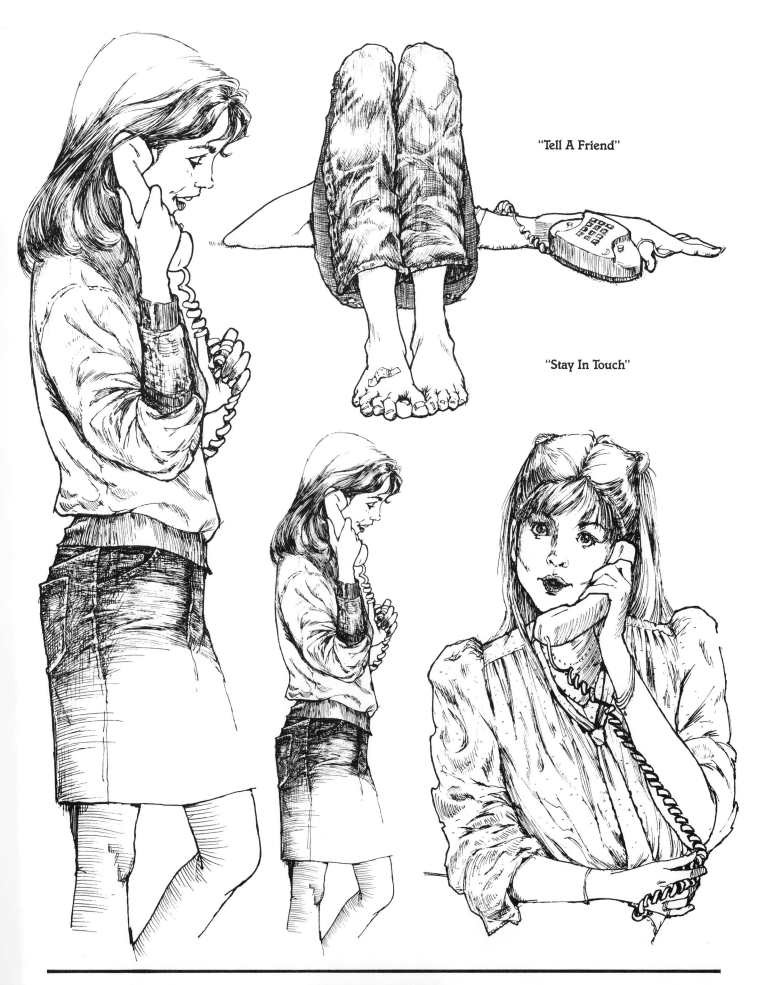

"Tell A Friend"

"Stay In Touch"

"Car Rally"

BE THERE

BE THERE

BE THERE

WATCH FOR...

WATCH FOR...

O GIVE THANKS

SENIOR GRADUATION

LONELINESS

UNDECIDED?

UNDECIDED?

MERRY

CHRISTMAS

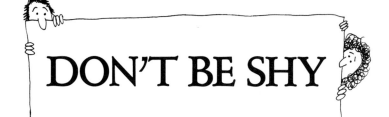

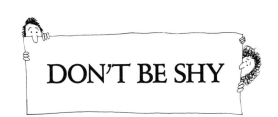

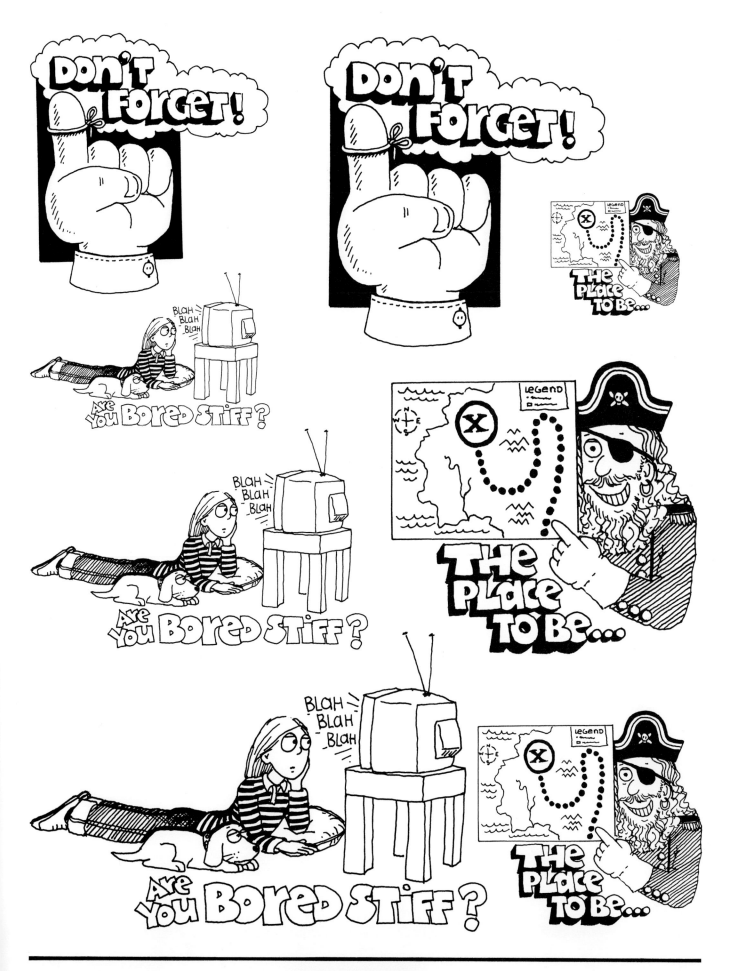

killer koaster

Graduation...

Graduation...

GO WOLVERINES!

BACK TO SCHOOL

killer koaster

"Bring A Friend"

"Movie Night"

"Adopt A Grandparent"

"Volleyball"

"Raft Trip"

"Swim Party"

"Beach Party"

Your
Announce-
ment
Here

YOUTH SPECIALTIES
CLIP-ART

"Parents"

"Self-Image" or
"Can't Decide?"

"Feel Trapped?"

"Treasure Hunt"

"Don't Worry"

"Are Your Parents A Little Up-Tight?"

"Mother-Daughter"

"Father-Son"

"Fun and Games"

"Self-Image"

"Welcome"

"Friendship"

"Spiritual Growth"

"Car Rally"

DON'T MISS THIS!

"Adopt A Grandparent"
"Helping Others"

Coming Events

Coming Events

Coming Events

Coming Events

WOW!

SUNDAY NIGHT

WOW!

SUNDAY NIGHT

WORSHIP

WORSHIP

WORSHIP

SUNDAY NIGHT

"Dating"

Dive into the Scriptures!

Dive into the Scriptures!

We missed you.

Please drop in next Sunday.

We missed you.

Please drop in next Sunday.

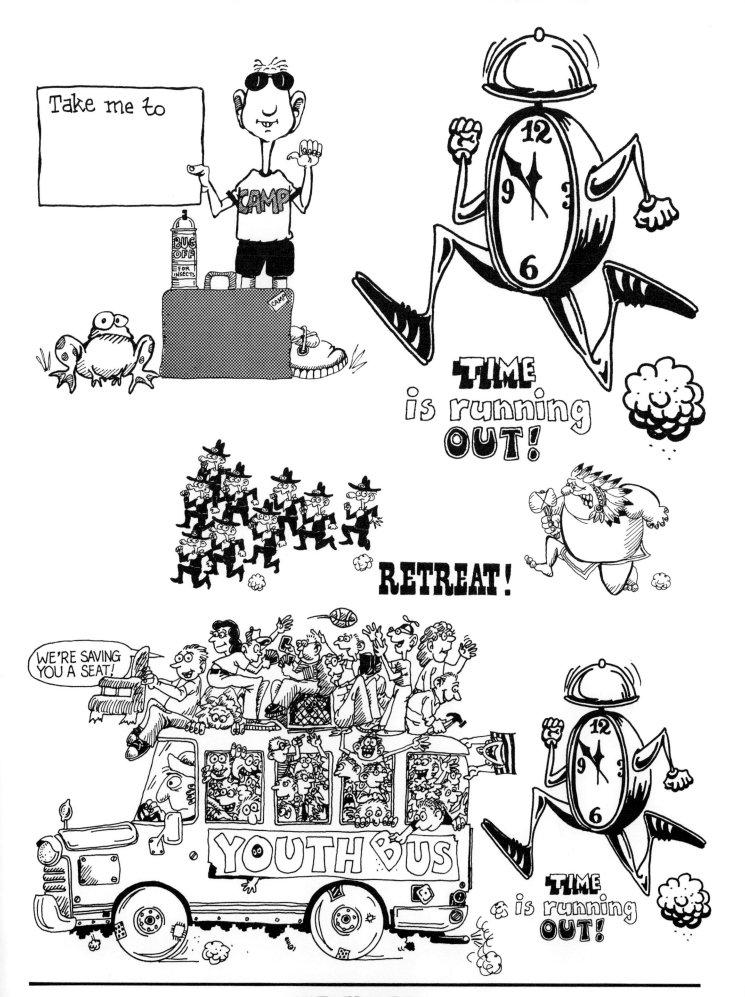

HOLY BIBLE

FALL
FLING

FALL
FLING

Memo:

IMPORTANT BULLETIN

IMPORTANT BULLETIN

PANCAKE BREAKFAST

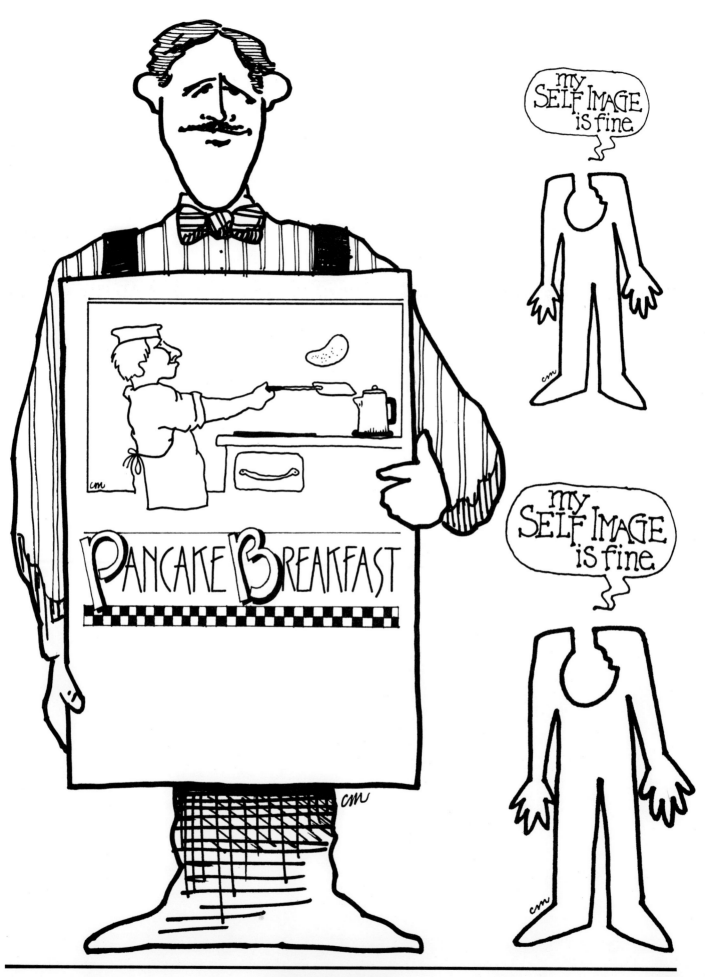

ROUND-UP

BIKE TRIP

BIG SUMMER
COOL DOWN
BASH!

THE BIKE TRIP

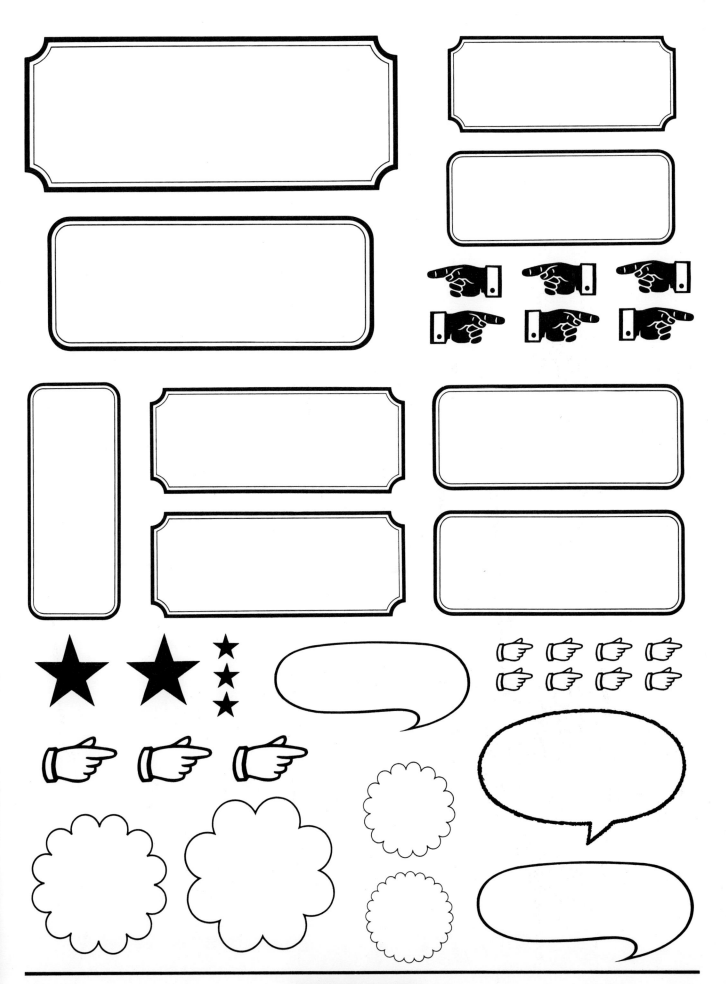

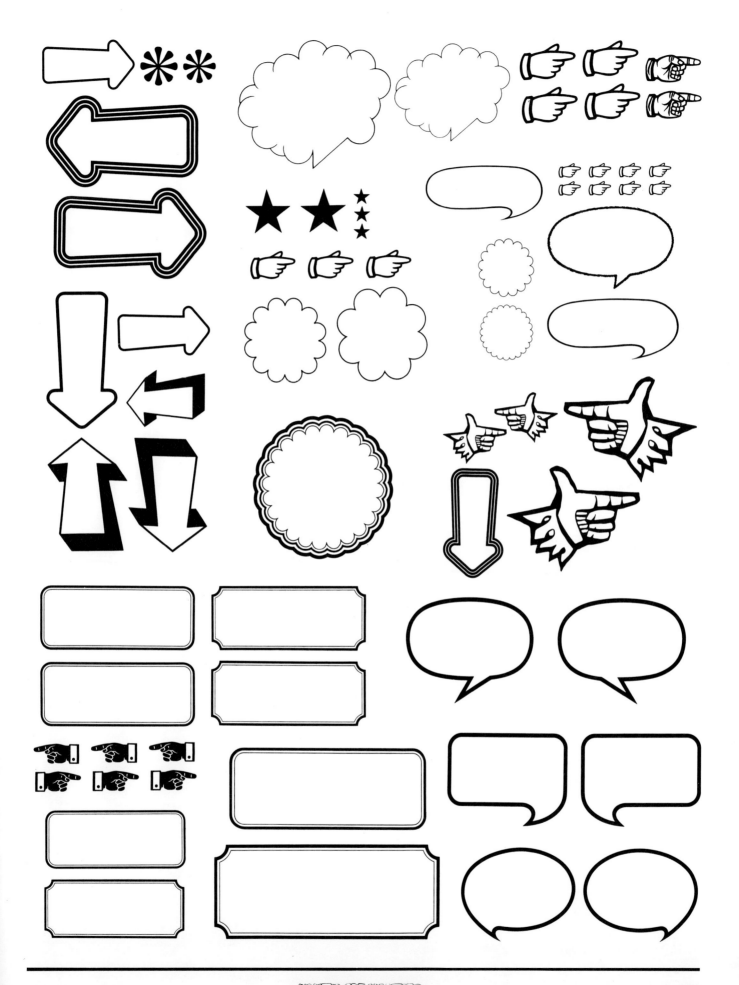

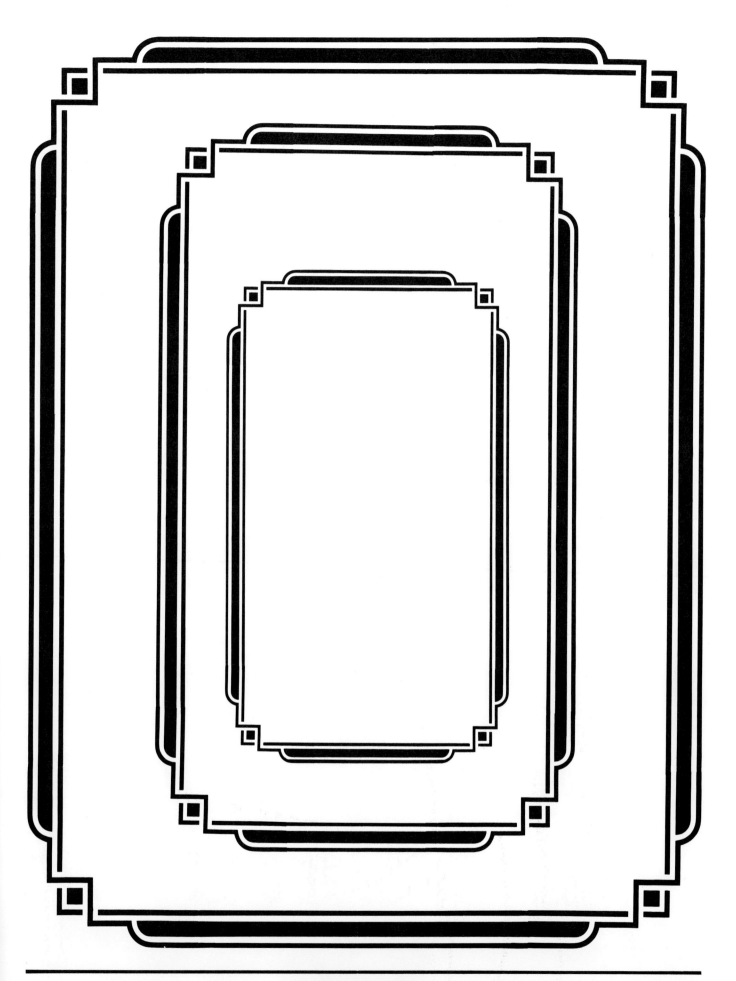

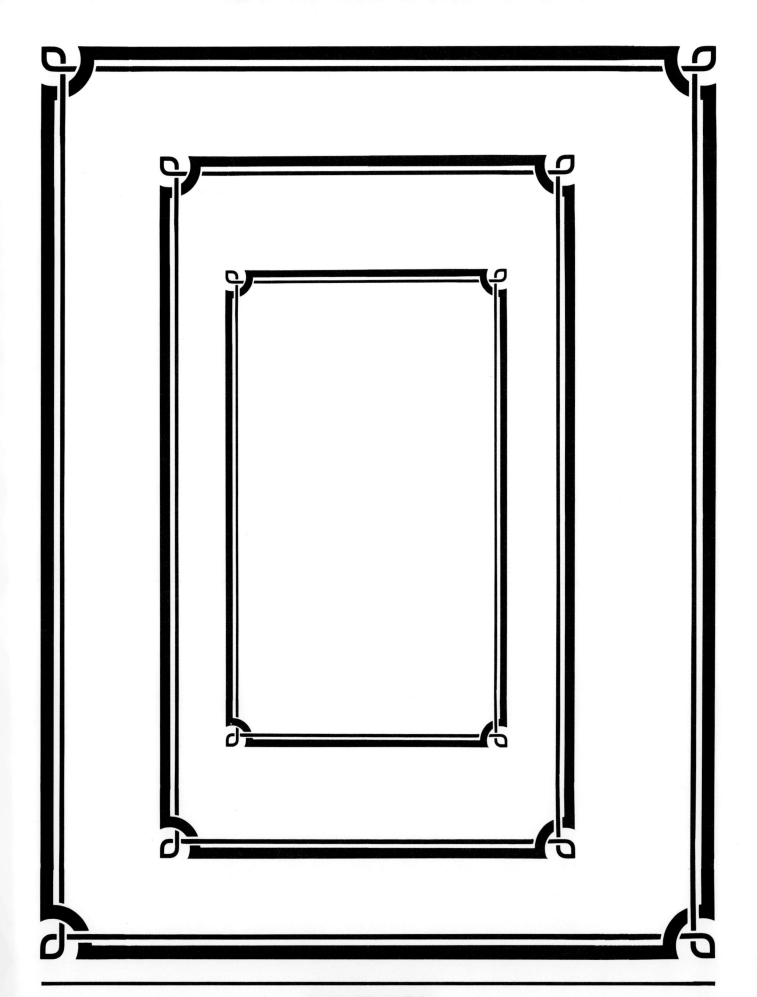

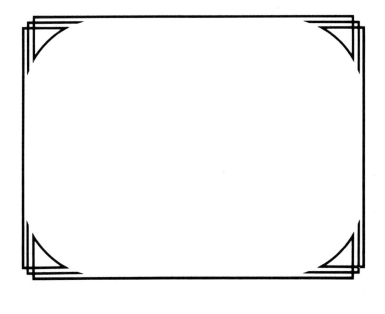

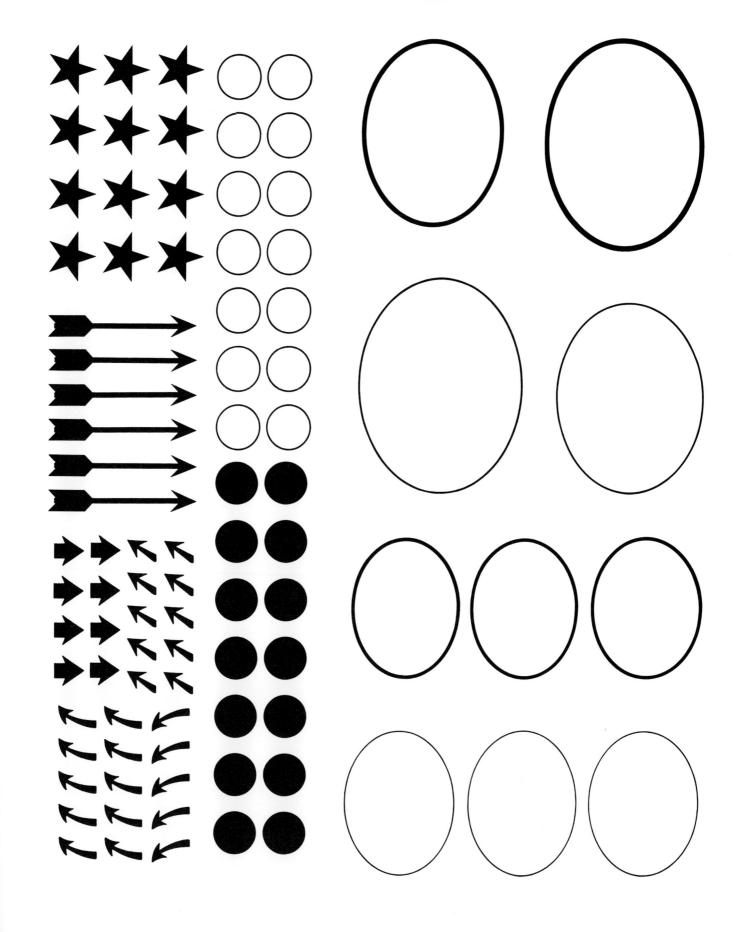

YOUTH SPECIALTIES CLIP-ART

Call for fast service:
(619) 440-2333

BUSINESS REPLY MAIL
FIRST CLASS   PERMIT NO. 16   EL CAJON, CA

POSTAGE WILL BE PAID BY ADDRESSEE

YOUTH SPECIALTIES
1224 Greenfield Dr.
El Cajon, CA 92021-9989

Call for fast service:
(619) 440-2333

NO POSTAGE
NECESSARY
IF MAILED
IN THE
UNITED STATES

BUSINESS REPLY MAIL
FIRST CLASS   PERMIT NO. 16   EL CAJON, CA

POSTAGE WILL BE PAID BY ADDRESSEE

YOUTH SPECIALTIES
1224 Greenfield Dr.
El Cajon, CA 92021-9989

The People Who Brought You This Book...

Please send me FREE information I've checked below:
☐ The Complete Youth Specialties Catalog of Youth Ministry Books and Products

Event Brochures:

☐ The National Youth Workers Convention

☐ The National Resource Seminar for Youth Workers

☐ "Grow For It" High School Events

☐ "On the Edge" Junior High Events

☐ "Understanding Your Teenager" Seminars for Parents

☐ "Riptide" Summer High School Conferences

Name _____

Address _____

City _____ State _____ Zip _____

The People Who Brought You This Book...

—————— *Invite you to discover MORE valuable youth ministry resources.* ——————

Youth Specialties offers an assortment of books, publications, tapes and events, all designed to encourage and train youth workers and their kids. Just check what you're interested in below and return this card, and we'll send you FREE information on our products and services.

Please send me FREE information I've checked below:
☐ The Complete Youth Specialties Catalog of Youth Ministry Books and Products

Event Brochures:

☐ The National Youth Workers Convention

☐ The National Resource Seminar for Youth Workers

☐ "Grow For It" High School Events

☐ "On the Edge" Junior High Events

☐ "Understanding Your Teenager" Seminars for Parents

☐ "Riptide" Summer High School Conferences

Name _____

Address _____

City _____ State _____ Zip _____

Coming Soon!

Super Summer!

Youth Group News

Here's What's Happening!

Don't Forget This!

CONGRATULATIONS!

Believe It or Not!

Incredible!

Next Week

This Week

Next Week Next Week This Week

Happy Birthday! **This Week**

Happy Birthday!   Happy Birthday!

From the Youth Pastor
From the Youth Pastor

Youth Group News
Youth Group News
Youth Group News

Don't Forget This!
Don't Forget This!
Don't Forget This!

CONGRATULATIONS!
CONGRATULATIONS!
CONGRATULATIONS!

Youth Ministry
Youth Ministry
Youth Ministry

Incredible!
Incredible!
Incredible!

Believe It or Not!
Believe It or Not!
Believe It or Not!

Mark It on Your Calendar!
Mark It on Your Calendar!
Mark It on Your Calendar!

NEWS
NEWS
NEWS

Food for Thought
Food for Thought
Food for Thought

Sing Along!
Sing Along!
Sing Along!

Super Summer!
Super Summer!
Super Summer!

Junior High

High School

College

Junior High

High School

College

Junior High

High School

College

Bring a Friend!

You Are Invited!

Bring a Friend!

You Are Invited!

Bring a Friend!

You Are Invited!

Don't Miss It!

Coming Soon!

Don't Miss It!

Coming Soon!

Don't Miss It!

Coming Soon!

Here's What's Happening!

In Person!

Here's What's Happening!

In Person!

Here's What's Happening!

In Person!

Special Guest

Sign Up Now!

Special Guest

Sign Up Now!

Special Guest

Sign Up Now!

Go For It!

Go For It!

Go For It!

LIGHT READING

News, Views & Who's Who in the Youth Group

Youth Group **News**

A·C·T·S
OF THE YOUTH GROUP

WOW

News, Views & Who's Who in the Youth Group

INDEX